MĀORI IN AOTEAROA NEW ZEALAND

Understanding the culture, protocols and customs

BUDDY MIKAERE

*E kore tatou e ngaro;
te kākano i ruia mai i Rangiātea.*

*We shall never be lost
for are we not the far-flung seed
of distant Rangiātea?*

WHITE CLOUD BOOKS

This edition published in 2023 by White Cloud Books, an imprint of Upstart Press Ltd.
First published in 2013 by New Holland Publishers (NZ) Ltd

Upstart Press Ltd.
26 Greenpark Road, Penrose, Auckland 1061,
New Zealand
www.upstartpress.co.nz

Copyright © 2023 in text: Buddy Mikaere
Copyright © 2023 in images: As credited on Page 64
Copyright © 2023 Upstart Press Ltd.

Buddy Mikaere has asserted his right to be identified as the author of this work.

ISBN: 978-1-990003-95-0

A catalogue record for this book is available from the National Library of New Zealand.

Front cover: (top) the karanga of welcome is given as part of the pōwhiri; (bottom left) a modern pou or carved post; (bottom centre) four generations on their marae; (bottom right) Taranaki-based kapa haka group Tuutuu Ka'ika perform in Hawera.
Rear cover: (top left) boys greet with a hongi; (top right) paddlers in a waka; (bottom) a carver at Te Puia in Rotorua.
Title page: (left) a modern pou or carved post; (centre) four generations on their marae; (right) Taranaki-based kapa haka group Tuutuu Ka'ika perform in Hawera.

10 9 8 7 6 5 4 3 2 1
Printed in China by 1010 Printing International Limited on paper sourced from sustainable forests

All rights reserved. No part of this publication may be reproduced, stored in a retrieval system or transmitted, in any form or by any means, electronic, mechanical, photocopying, recording or otherwise, without the prior written permission of the publishers and copyright holders.

AUTHOR'S NOTE

The ceremonials described in this book are the ones that I am familiar with and which make up the tikanga, customary practices, followed by the descendants of the *Mataatua* ancestral canoe. There are of course many local variations depending on hapū and iwi affiliations and the various tikanga that they consider fitting, but the practices described here hold true for most contemporary Māori communities.

CONTENTS

ORIGINS OF NGĀ TĀNGATA, THE PEOPLE — 6
Long journey to the sunrise — 6
Polynesian voyaging — 8
Following in Kupe's wake — 9
Aotearoa: a strange new land — 10

TRADITIONAL MĀORI SOCIETY — 12
Whānau, hapū and iwi — 12
War and utu, revenge — 14
Kāinga and pā — 15
Climate and resources — 17
Whakairo, carving — 19
Wharenui — 20
Waka taua — 20
Tā moko, tattooing — 21
The traditional world — 23

CONTACT: WORLDS IN COLLISION — 24
Trade — 24
Guns and warfare — 25
Missionaries and literacy — 26
The Treaty of Waitangi and nationhood — 27
Conflict with government — 28
Resistance and religion — 28
Defeat and loss — 30
Resilience and growth — 30
Drift to the cities — 32
Intermarriage and migration — 33

CONTEMPORARY MĀORI SOCIETY — 34
Marae — 34
Contemporary Māori ritual — 36
Pōwhiri: accommodating visitors — 37
Hui: meetings on the marae — 41
Tangi: funeral — 42

THE RENAISSANCE OF MĀORI CULTURE — 48
Te reo: the Māori language — 48
Kapa haka: performing arts — 48
Māori music — 51
Haka — 52
Waka ama — 53
Contemporary tā moko — 54
Art and crafts — 56

THE FUTURE — 58
Appendix A: The National Anthem — 60
Appendix B: The 'Ka Mate' Haka — 60
Glossary — 60
Image credits — 64

PREVIOUS PAGE: *Waka taua.*

LEFT: *Gable figure, Papawai marae, Wairarapa.*

ORIGINS OF **NGĀ TĀNGATA,** THE PEOPLE

IT'S A LONG, LONG WAY from mainland China to the rocky headland which marks the place where the Whakatāne River joins with the great sea, Kiwa's ocean. But that is the journey my ancestors completed about eight hundred years ago when our ancestral waka Mataatua *crossed the bar at the river mouth and they stepped ashore.*

OPPOSITE TOP: *The landing place of the* Mataatua *ancestral canoe at Whakatāne Heads. The stylised statue of a woman (opposite left) set on a rock at the entrance to the harbour commemorates the story of the ancestress Wairaka, who, in the absence of the male crew of the* Mataatua *canoe, had to perform a man's job – 'whaka tāne' – to save the canoe from drifting away.*

OPPOSITE RIGHT: *The gateway face mask is a typical example of the stylised form followed by Māori wood carving.*

LONG JOURNEY TO THE SUNRISE

Sometime in the forgotten past, the forebears of the people who came on the *Mataatua* had made their way down to the waters that separated the Southeast Asian mainland from the island archipelagos and the myriad land specks that make up the steamy jungle islands of Micronesia and Melanesia. They set off across the sea and over aeons journeyed through the island-strewn ocean before reaching what we know now as Western Polynesia.

From there they set out east towards the sunrise and Eastern Polynesia as far as the furthest islands: Rapanui (Easter Island), Hawai'i of the fire, the high places of Te Fenua (the Marquesas) and Tahiti, with nearby sacred Rai'atea Island, which is believed by many to be the ancient religious heart of the Polynesian world. That sense of a beating Polynesian heart is captured today in the whakataukī or proverb which Māori use to remind themselves of their chiefly descent and origins:

| **E kore tatou e ngaro; te kākano i ruia mai i Rangiātea.** | We shall never be lost, for are we not the far-flung seed of distant Rangiātea |

Some say that these fearless travellers of the great ocean reached as far as the brooding coastline of the land we now call South America. The evidence for their journey to and from that land is found in what the people came to regard as the food of the gods: the tubers of the kūmara or sweet potato. The kūmara

homeland is Central and South America, and a return journey is the only sensible way to explain how Polynesians possessed this valuable food source.

Other evidence says that the patterns in the languages of these early Polynesians are derived from a common source called proto-Austronesian, which is also evidence that they share their roots with the people of the strange island of Madagascar off the eastern coast of Africa. Echoes of that ancient language can still be traced by linguists. Unlike the kūmara, no traditions or physical evidence survives, but it does suggest a lost one-way journey by our ancestors to the far west, following the setting sun.

We belong then to that enormous upwelling of humanity that came out of the Asian mainland, and we retain in our cultural genes some faint echoes of those origins. The importance of whānau, family; reverence for the ancestors and genealogy; tattooing as a means of bodily adornment; the curving spiral design line; gardening and the growing of cultivated crops are all cultural features that come from our ancient Asian homeland.

POLYNESIAN VOYAGING

But the travellers who I imagine stepping ashore on a sunny morning at Whakatāne Heads didn't know they had reached the end of their particular epic journey. To them – and to those who had completed the same journey earlier, or who followed later – journeying to faraway places was just a normal part of the great cycle of Polynesian life. Travels from one island to another were made in the sure belief that the great ocean was full of islands and there would be another just below the stationary cloud on the horizon that marked it, or whose lagoon they could see reflected off the overhead cloud cover.

To find land all they needed to do was follow the seabird flocks home at sunset, look for floating seaweed in the water, or mark the set of the waves whose patterned march across the sea had been disrupted by striking land. Better still was to follow the sailing directions of previous voyagers and find the stars at night which stood over those islands, then sail down the wind to that place.

On the map you can see that Aotearoa New Zealand lies in the far south-west corner of the Pacific. It is almost as far away from anywhere else as you can get. Yet when other peoples came to settle here, towards the end of the eighteenth century, they found the land inhabited by Māori, a virile warrior people with a lifestyle adapted to the environment, its resources and the cool temperate climate that they had mastered.

We don't know for sure, but we can assume that the vessels in which the ancestors travelled were

double-hulled waka — similar to the big oceangoing proa or prau that you can still find in parts of Micronesia and the Malayan Archipelago.

Some say that our ancestors were castaways, sent here on the winds and waves of the tropical storms that sometimes drift south out of the central Pacific. But we say no. We say that our ancestors deliberately sailed here, refugees fleeing from the violent tensions that overpopulation of the 'home' islands inevitably brought.

FOLLOWING IN KUPE'S WAKE

We say that our people came to the land that the mischievous demi-god Māui, known to all the Pacific peoples, fished up out of the sea using a hook made from the jawbone of his grandmother and baited with his own blood. The giant fish he drew from the depths was Te Ika a Māui — Māui's fish — known today as the North Island. The shape of the fish, with its long tail pointing to the north, is clear from any map you care to look at. The 'fishing up' of course was a metaphor for discovery and describes the land rising into view from over the horizon.

We also say that our people came in the wake of the famous explorer Kupe, who, like the mythical Māui, was in pursuit of fish. But Kupe's 'fish' was a giant wheke, octopus, which he eventually trapped and slaughtered in the swift currents of Raukawa, Cook Strait, before returning home with the sailing directions that would allow the people to replicate his journey.

Another version says that Kupe's journey was in fact yet another eternal triangle saga, with Kupe in pursuit of his wife Kura Marotina, who had been stolen away by his younger brother Hoturapa. We can be sure that Kupe caught up with the lovers because his name lives on, while that of his brother has almost been extinguished.

ABOVE: *A waka taua — war canoe — under way. Tourists are often invited to join the crew for a unique experience.*

OPPOSITE TOP: *A stylised whale tail at Takahanga Marae, Kaikoura. Kaikoura is internationally renowned for its whale-watching activities.*

OPPOSITE LOWER: *This modern double-hulled fishing canoe is a small echo of the giant ocean-going vessels that brought Māori to Aotearoa.*

Ka tito au,	I sing,
Ka tito au,	I sing,
Ka tito au ki a Kupe,	I sing of Kupe
Te tangata nana	The man who
I hoehoea te moana	Paddled over the seas,
I topetopea te whenua.	And cut the islands from the main.
Tū ke a Kapiti,	Who set Kapiti Island apart,
Tū ke a Mana,	Who severed Mana from the land,
Tū ke Arapawa;	And Arapawa;
Ko ngā tohu ēnā	These are the signs
A taku tupuna, a Kupe . . .	Of the deeds of my ancestor Kupe . . .

When the pressure of too many people on too small a land area – the homeland of Hawaiki – became too much, some of our people remembered the journey of Kupe and set off for the land that he had found and returned from. According to our traditions they battled storms, whirlpools, monsters, thirst and hunger but finally found the land – Aotearoa, the land of the long white cloud, as Kupe had so aptly named it.

Nowadays we jet between New Zealand and the island nations of Western Samoa, the Cook Islands and Tahiti in a matter of hours. But for our ancestors it was a giant leap of faith to set out in their fragile vessels, armed only with their sailing skills and a belief in Kupe's thin folio of sailing instructions, a legacy of their ancestral heritage. We can only marvel at the fact that some survived that hazardous journey of around 4000 kilometres, and speculate on the uncounted who must have been lost forever in the ocean's vastness.

AOTEAROA: A STRANGE NEW LAND

And what a strange new land they found. It held a mixture of natural riches, but was set in a climate far different to where they had come from. The riches were in the resources that their Neolithic culture needed and which the homeland islands of the Pacific lacked. Here was a wealth of better timber resources – hardwoods in particular – for house and boat building; harder stone for the manufacture of tools, weapons and ornaments. Here was a land flowing with water, where the air and forests were thick with birds – some of them giants, like the moa; rivers, streams, lakes; an ocean teeming with fish, and estuaries and shorelines rich in easily gathered shellfish; safe harbours and anchorages; but, most of all, space, living room – room to grow, room for people.

These first settlers followed the patterns of life with which they were familiar, preferring settlement close to the coast and usually in association with a stream or river mouth for drinking water. Their midden remnants – rubbish heaps – show they soon latched on to the moa as an important food source; and, not surprisingly, the giant birds were rendered extinct within a relatively short time. Fish bones show that the settlers continued to target mostly reef fish, as they had in the reef-fringed islands from which they had come, until they learned to adapt their techniques to capturing the local species.

The tapa bark cloth clothing they used in the tropics was too light for local conditions, and over time heavier clothing made from harakeke, flax, which was pounded into weavable fibre, became the replacement.

But the need for radical adjustment came with their gardening efforts. The more temperate climate with its cold coastal winds and pesky bird crop-raiders like the pūkeko and weka made horticulture a risky business. Gardens had to be located within the shelter of forest clearings or behind stone walls or stick fences. Gravel was added to the soil in some places to raise temperatures and enable a longer growing season because the seasonal nature of the climate allowed only one crop per year.

It was far from idyllic; in fact, for these first settlers, life was short and brutal and the battle to survive was unrelenting. However, it bred resilience and stoicism in their approach to hardship; character traits that were remarked on by early nineteenth-century European visitors. But up until the arrival of tauiwi, foreigners, we thought ourselves to be the only people in the whole world and we called ourselves after our word for ordinary: Māori – humans.

ABOVE: *Gathering toheroa at Oreti Beach, Murihiku or Southland. Toheroa are the largest of New Zealand's clam species.*

BELOW: *A kete – flax basket – containing tuangi (cockles) and pipi (with elongated shells). These clam species are the country's most numerous and can be found in estuaries.*

TRADITIONAL MĀORI SOCIETY

MĀORI SOCIETY WAS THEN – and still is now – very much kin-based. The first settlers would have been organised into whānau (extended family groups), which with time grew into hapū (a grouping of whānau), and finally into iwi or tribes (a loose confederation of hapū based on their descent from a common ancestor). Tribes are sometimes spoken of as forming a confederation – a waka – on the basis that they share the same ancestral canoe, but this is thought to be a relatively modern construct.

WHĀNAU, HAPŪ AND IWI

Tribes might infrequently form alliances to defend or invade a common territory or for big communal tasks such as making and using giant nets for seasonal fishing. But it was the hapū rather than the iwi that formed the dominant political, economic and social entity.

Leadership

Whānau and hapū were led by rangatira or chiefs, the positions often being inherited through a senior line of descent. Individuals could also rise to prominence and positions of leadership through personal characteristics, based largely on their fighting skills in physical or strategic terms. The hapū in its role as the political unit, along with other closely related hapū, might constitute an iwi grouping and accept the nominal leadership of an ariki, an overall chief in time of war. But such alliances were mostly short-lived and usually succumbed to petty rivalries and tensions. Leadership in these situations required great skills of persuasion and diplomacy in order to weld a group together to achieve unity of purpose. But independence of action was a quality highly sought after and exercised by rangatira as a demonstration of their mana or personal prestige.

The need for such skills soon became apparent. As the population in Aotearoa grew and competition for resources and living space increased – particularly where the climate was gentler and the soil more fertile – warfare became inevitable, even among closely related hapū and tribes. It was a warrior society where land and, more importantly, resources were gained by strength of arms.

OPPOSITE TOP: *In this early painting by August Earle, depicting traditional life, a Ngāpuhi chief standing on the thwarts of a waka taua (war canoe) addresses his followers – possibly as a precursor to a war expedition.*

OPPOSITE LOWER: *This group of Tūhoe people at Te Umuroa near Ruātahuna in the Urewera country are obviously posed for the photograph, but the setting is illustrative of rural life in the mid to late 1800s.*

13

WAR AND UTU, REVENGE

It was also a society driven by utu – revenge – where chiefly mana could be easily offended and friendships turned to bitter enmity in the blink of an eye. Utu could be satisfied with gifts of land or women, but more often only bloodshed would do. Payback killings created feuds that lasted for generations, to the point where the original offence had long since faded from memory as each payback created a new future grievance.

This unrelenting cycle of utu trapped Māori in a cultural dead-end because of the focus placed on achieving revenge and the wasteful use of energy, resources and lives in its pursuit. Escape from the cycle came only with outside intervention at the end of the eighteenth century and contact with a new world-view which, despite its many failings, had an underpinning religious philosophy, Christianity, that made virtues of forgiveness, mercy and compassion. Christianity also sought to modify behaviour through social controls exercised by the establishment and implementation of an objective law code.

Weaponry

Warriors fought with weapons made from wood, bone and stone: tao, spears, with fire-hardened points; taiaha, quarterstaffs, with an elaborately carved point at one end that meant they could also be used as thrusting weapons; long-handled clubs known as tewhatewha, made of wood or whalebone; and an assortment of short-handled striking clubs with flat, hooked or violin-shaped blades. An expert could use a stone mere, club, to stun an opponent and then crush or remove the top of the skull with an upward sweep of the arm.

Men gloried in war. It could take place at any time, but fighting expeditions were usually set down for late summer after the meagre crops had been harvested and other foods gathered in, preserved and stored – and before the bad weather of winter came, making travel difficult. ■

KĀINGA AND PĀ

The undefended kāinga, settlements, which the people normally occupied on a seasonal basis so they could more easily tend their gardens or gather and dry fish, shellfish and other foods, were abandoned in times of war. The people retreated to places of refuge – the pā, Māori forts, comprehensive structures which consisted of a series of living terraces protected by ditches, banks and wooden palisades. The palisades were erected with much labour: the timber had to be cut and dragged to the site, then laboriously dug into place, and the whole was lashed together with flax ropes that required frequent renewal.

We can still see the remnant earthworks of many such pā atop steep ridges, hills or cliffs, places that offered expansive views of the surrounding countryside and where the topography could be cleverly exploited to contribute to the strength of the defences. The scale and complexity of some of these pā fortifications is impressive and they represent the furthest advance of Māori engineering.

LEFT: *Two leading rangatira of Tūhoe, Hurae Puketapu (left) and Te Whenuanui alongside the palisades at Mataatua Pā, Ruatāhuna. Hurae Puketapu was an informant of ethnographer Elsdon Best while Te Whenuanui was among the early leaders protesting the confiscation of Tūhoe land.*

OPPOSITE: *Modern wooden patu, or club.*

Houses within the pā

The terraces within the pā were used for house and storage sites and sometimes, if space permitted, small gardens. The houses were simple constructions: a rectangular wooden framework lashed together, anchored to house posts, the whole thatched with the palm-like leaves of the nīkau or bundles of raupō, bulrushes. A rock hearth at the far end provided a fireplace for heating, and smoke could escape through a hole in the roof. A small door demanded a crouched entry, which meant that an enemy forcing his way in could be easily despatched. The houses themselves were usually partly sunken into the earth as a means of retaining warmth in winter. Bedding was piles of bracken and grasses on sleeping platforms. Early Pākehā (European) visitors found the houses smoky, hot and stuffy and a haven for hordes of fleas.

A chief's house might have carved outward-facing wall panels on all sides, a small window and sometimes a porch space at the entrance – a place to sit and work on wet days. Such a house would normally occupy the tihi, the highest point within the pā, and have an open space in front of it – the marae ātea – which was a gathering place for the people.

Wharenui

While the chief's house – normally the largest house in the pā – might be used for gatherings, a purpose-built communal meeting house or wharenui was sometimes constructed for this purpose. The size of the house and the elaborateness of its decoration were physical statements of the wealth and mana, prestige, of the people who owned it.

BELOW: *Modern-day wharenui at Te Kaha.*

OPPOSITE TOP: *A pātaka— this storehouse is one of the featured buildings in the reconstructed pā at Whakarewarewa in Rotorua.*

OPPOSITE LOWER: *Sorting kūmara in Northland at the turn of the twentieth century. The kūmara were dug up and left to 'sweat' – lose excess moisture under the pulled-out vines so that their skins could harden before being stored.*

Pātaka: storehouses

Richly decorated pātaka, storehouses, were built on poles so that their contents could be kept safe and dry from weather, from kiore – Polynesian rats – and possibly also from hungry kinsmen. These pātaka served a double purpose: firstly, as storehouse and warehouse; and, secondly, like the communal wharenui, they were symbols of the power and mana of their owners. A fancy pātaka bespoke a wealth of resources and was a physical statement about the competency and industriousness of the owners as food gatherers.

CLIMATE AND RESOURCES
Agriculture

The resources that were stored included fish dried by sun and wind, strings of dried or smoked shellfish, birds cooked and potted in their own fat in hue (gourds) or in inflated kelp bladders, and bundles of fernroot. Kūmara tubers were stored on piles of bracken in covered pits. The pits often had their own drainage system to ensure the kūmara and other goods stored inside remained dry.

The climate here was cooler, wetter and with more defined seasons than in the Islands; and in some parts of the country winter brought strong winds, frost and snow. The few domesticated plants that were brought in the waka struggled to survive. It was not a case of just putting plants in the ground and letting warm soils and sun do their magic, as was the case in the homeland islands. Only the hardy taro, the hue and, with much labour, the kūmara made up the lean but important cropping list.

A slash-and-burn gardening technique was practised: the cleared brushwood was burnt and the ash mixed into the soil to aid fertility. Once that fertility was exhausted the gardens were simply moved to a fresh location nearby and the whole process was repeated.

The length of the growing season for kūmara could be extended in cooler regions by the addition of sand and gravel to help open up and warm the

soils to enable earlier planting. The sand and gravel were dug from pits and carried to the garden plots where it was evenly spread.

The young kūmara plants might be covered with brush at night if there was a chance of a frost, and each plant was given an earthen mound and watered individually by the laborious hauling of water in gourd containers or bark buckets. Not surprisingly, the warmer northern parts of the country were also the most densely populated (and hence the most fought over) because of their more favourable growing conditions.

Fibre and clothing

The aute or paper mulberry bush also came – though it has not survived here. Back in Hawaiki its bark was beaten and made into tapa cloth, but in the new land more robust coverings were needed. Kilts and cloaks made from woven flax fibre became the norm. Some of these cloaks were laboriously fixed with bird feathers or trimmed with dogskin fur: these were highly prestigious garments for chiefs, and represented the pinnacle of the weaver's art. It was said that when a chief put on his dogskin cloak it was a sign that he was going to war.

Woven flax cloak with kiwi feather fringe.

Rat and dog

Two mammals – the kiore and the kurī, the Māori dog – accompanied the first settlers. Both animals were also a valued source of meat. Kiore, which have a mainly vegetarian diet, were captured in elaborate traps laid along their pathways through the bush and up ridges. Dogs served as watchkeepers and helped with settlement garbage disposal by scavenging for scraps. They also provided valued meat for important guests; and their bones were used to make fish hooks and small tools like chisels.

WHAKAIRO, CARVING

In all Pacific cultures whakairo, carving, in wood, stone or bone, has a special place. Carving provides a focus for design and artistic expression. But Māori took whakairo work to an entirely different level in comparison to the rest of Polynesia. The intricate designs and patterns they brought to even commonplace items turned those objects into works of art – functional and beautiful at the same time.

One reason for the flowering of whakairo in Aotearoa was the availability of a wider range of stone materials for the manufacture of carving tools. Skilled woodcarvers used chisels and adzes made from basalt, argillite, obsidian or, best of all, nephrite jade or pounamu – greenstone – to make carvings which were initially small and simple but which often possessed an inner force that belied their humble origins. In time, powerful images imbued with great spiritual power were created. These became the templates for the artistic drive behind nearly all Māori wooden imagery.

The images depicted were those of atua, powerful ancestors who had achieved deity status. These carvings became larger and increasingly intricate over time – particularly in the detail of surface decoration – as the artists' familiarity with the new hardwoods and tools grew. The prestige of their chiefly sponsors demanded works that depicted the power and influence of their ancestors, thereby adding to their own mana.

The simple notching or straight-lined designs that were brought from Polynesia gave way, over time, to curvilinear designs of increasing complexity. The development of the intricate double spiral pattern is a good example of the unique designs that have set Māori whakairo apart from other carved work across the Pacific.

BELOW LEFT: *An ancestral figure is an example of North Island east coast carving.*

BELOW: *An ancestral pou – post or pole – from the Te Arawa people of Rotorua.*

WHARENUI

The wharenui provided a convenient display space for the confident expression of whakairo work. Houses became elaborately carved, replete with poupou, standing ancestral wall figures, and richly carved centreposts and bargeboards and door lintels. These pieces became so revered that in times of danger they might be dismantled and hidden in caves or buried in a convenient swamp. These houses also featured painted rafters decorated with intricate kōwhaiwhai patterns, based on the graceful curving fern fronds of the forest; and tukutuku wall panels – woven reed screens with decorative designs. Along with the richly carved pātaka, wharenui became physical symbols of the prosperity and wealth of the people to whom they belonged.

WAKA TAUA

The availability of hardwood timber enabled another physical expression of power and mana: the richly carved waka taua or war canoe – the ultimate Māori war machine. The rise of the waka taua was to an extent the direct result of the shorter journeys and calmer harbours and coastal waters. While the double-hulled sailing canoes were retained for some

time – we know they were still used in the seventeenth century – single-hulled vessels became the norm (sometimes with an outrigger for added stability). The big single-hulled waka taua, capable of carrying crew of up to a hundred men, represented the peak of Māori maritime development.

As with all accoutrements of war, the waka taua was designed to intimidate. Its appearance was enhanced by a tauihu or prow with a carving of a fierce ancestral face, and a high taurapa or sternpost trailing feathered streamers – all designed to add to the majesty of the vessel as it glided effortlessly by.

The labour involved in building a waka was immense. A suitable tree was felled using fire and stone axes. It was roughly shaped and the interior was hollowed out by adzing, chiselling and burning. The rough hull was then dragged, using ropes and rollers, out of the forest to the nearest body of water for testing and finishing. The work took many months and, as with many aspects of Māori life, was surrounded with religious ritual designed to ensure the success of the project and to protect those working on the waka from spiritual harm.

TĀ MOKO, TATTOOING

It was not just wood that was carved: in common with traditions found all around the Pacific, people were carved too. The faces and bodies of chiefs, especially, were living canvases for tā moko, the Māori practice and art of tattooing. Facial

OPPOSITE TOP: *A modern warrior strikes a pose inside the wharenui.*

OPPOSITE LOWER: *The crew of a waka taua provide a salute with their raised hoe or paddles.*

BELOW: *Acquisition of moko. This painting by the soldier artist Horatio Robley shows the very painful face moko carving operation. The tōhunga or priestly expert is holding a bone chisel in his left hand while in his right he holds a light stick which is used to tap the chisel and drive the point home.*

designs consisted of elaborate spirals, whorls and patterns with individual designs of sufficient uniqueness to be a discussion point: often a man could be identified from his moko, even though he might not be personally known. In later contact times, after Pākehā arrived, a chief who had not learned to read and write would draw the main element of his facial tattoo on a document in lieu of his signature. The buttocks and upper thighs of men were also chiselled with raperape and pūhoro patterns, the decorative elements expected of a warrior chief.

Tattooing rituals

The process of tattooing could take many months and, like all highly personal and important events of a chief's life, was surrounded by religious ritual to ensure success. Because a moko design, for example, involved working on the most sacred part of a person's body – the head – it was important that the artist be protected from the tapu or personal spirituality of the recipient. Other rituals were designed to ward off ill will that might mean the work would be marred in some way. Great personal humiliation was the lot of a person whose moko design was crooked or not symmetrical. Other rituals were to help the person being tattooed cope with the many weeks of pain that would have to be endured before the work was done.

Acquisition of moko. A tōhunga working on a woman recipient of a chin and lip moko. The procedure and the pain involved is the same as for men. This might be a study posed for the camera rather than an actual operation.

The tattooing process

The design was first drawn on using charcoal, and the outline was tapped out using a light, sharp needle. Small chisels made of bone or stone were then used to dig out the flesh to a depth of 1–2 millimetres. The greenish blue, sometimes black colouration of all moko came from use of an 'ink' made by mixing soot with oil or fat and the burnt residue of a particular caterpillar associated with the tōtara tree. Chisels and needles were dipped into this ink mixture, or sometimes it was rubbed directly into the carved flesh.

Women of chiefly status sometimes carried the moko on the lower lip and chin.

A family group from about 1910 at the Tūhoe kāinga of Te Umuroa – probably dressed in their best clothes, with the man in the shadow of the porch wearing a fine feather kākahu or cloak.

THE TRADITIONAL WORLD

The traditional lifestyle in Aotearoa could never be described as easy – and it was far from the romantic idyll portrayed by later travellers to the Pacific. With lots of hard work and good fortune it was possible for people to survive – to flourish even – but the reality was that life for most was harsh, short and often brutal. A man was middle-aged by the time he reached thirty-five, and was reckoned an old man in his late forties – by which time hard toil had bent his limbs and an unrelenting diet consisting largely of pounded and roasted gritty fernroot had ground down his teeth.

And that might have been it, the sum total of Māori life: Māori would have continued to be just another tribal society eking out a living on the edge of the world, devoid of contact with the great currents of change that had swept the known world, and bereft of new ideas and new technologies. Except that in the 1642 a timid Dutch trader, Abel Tasman, came over the horizon, saw the green hills of a new land, and suffered the indignity of having one of his boat crews massacred and in all likelihood eaten by the locals. He named the land he had found New Zealand, and promptly fled back to Batavia where the Dutch had built a trading colony.

But he added a new wavy line to the map of the known world; and 127 years later, in 1769, the more resolute Englishman Lieutenant James Cook of HMS *Endeavour* came to give Tasman's wavy line a surer cartographic picture, and in so doing he changed the traditional Māori world forever. ■

CONTACT: WORLDS IN COLLISION

IN THE SPACE OF JUST 100 YEARS, from roughly 1769 into the 1860s, the traditional lifestyle and much of the thinking that went with it was swept away as Neolithic Māori society ran full tilt into the Victorian world of the Industrial Revolution. At first the lifestyle changes were incremental and therefore manageable. The numbers of new people arriving in the late eighteenth and early nineteenth centuries were few and their impact was relatively minor. The reports and scientific papers published after the exploratory visits of Tasman and Cook aroused much interest in Europe. Among the first visitors were sealers and whalers, who came in search of skins and oil. These early visitors marked the beginning of the social intercourse between Māori and Pākehā.

TRADE

With the establishment of the convict settlements in New South Wales on the east coast of Australia in 1788, contact in New Zealand expanded to meet the trading opportunities offered by the needs of those settlements and the sailing ships that supplied them. The initial items sought by the first trading visitors were timber and, most importantly, flax for the manufacture of rope and cordage. The Royal Navy sent ships to survey the coastline but also in search of wooden spars and masts from the coastal forests that Cook had so much admired and reported on.

Māori soon developed a commercial enterprise supplying visiting ships with fish, pork and potatoes. This trade grew exponentially when sealing and whaling operations began, and more and more ships visited the northern parts of the country to provision en route to the southern whaling and sealing grounds. The ships normally called in again on their return to stock up for the homeward journey.

Cultivation of the potato – which was introduced to New Zealand by Cook and other earlier visitors – had an enormous impact on Māori society in several ways. Kūmara was almost completely abandoned as a crop, replaced by the hardy potato, which grew easily almost everywhere and required minimal care and labour. This new source of carbohydrate also ousted fernroot, which had been

A painting of a dramatic haka from the 1850s by the English artist William Strutt who lived briefly in Taranaki. This painting is probably based on the beach at New Plymouth. The warriors have both traditional and European weapons and clothing.

the staple up until that time and which required roasting, pounding, shaping into rough gritty cakes and then cooking, whereas potatoes grew like weeds and could be plucked from the ground and eaten raw or cooked.

Pigs were also introduced by Cook: they thrived and soon produced large mobs which supplied the trade markets as well as being a welcome protein addition to the Māori diet.

GUNS AND WARFARE

Some things did not change. As in traditional times, once provision for the winter larder had been made, it was time to go to war – and the traders in particular brought new ways for Māori to kill each other. Māori learnt early and quickly about the deadly power of firearms; and some tribes were armed for offensive purposes as early as 1806. The pursuit of the new weaponry became a priority for the war ambitions of chiefs, and this opportunity to expand saw a shift in Māori society: the people were pressed into the drudgery of gathering and preparing tons of flax and the new wonder crop, potatoes, to barter for often poorly manufactured muskets.

From about 1818 through to the mid 1830s armed war parties, taua, raided up and down the North Island. Those who possessed muskets in particular exercised a fearsome toll on the tribes who still relied on traditional weapons such as clubs and spears.

ABOVE: *The missionary Creed family arrives in Taranaki in 1844 as imagined by George Baxter, a London-based artist who never visited New Zealand. The overly dressed Māori women depicted carrying Mrs Creed ashore is one of several inaccuracies.*

OPPOSITE: *A group of visitors in front of the Treaty House at Waitangi in the Bay of Islands.*

MISSIONARIES AND LITERACY

In June 1814 the first mission station was established by the Church Missionary Society in the Bay of Islands. The missionaries brought the gospel and, more importantly, they opened up more trade opportunities. In fact from the Māori perspective the missionaries' message was secondary to their usefulness as contact points for trading purposes, including the trade in firearms.

Eventually, by the mid 1830s the tribes reached arms parity. The Christian message took on a new importance as the tribes who had armed themselves early and wreaked widespread destruction now sought to avoid threats of utu, revenge, by claiming to live under the protection of Jesus Christ and the mana of peace.

Power of the written word

This transition away from the warrior lifestyle brought with it a new perception of the power of the written word; and in this same period in the 1830s there was a surge in the desire to acquire literacy, hand in hand with widespread conversion to Christianity. The missionaries and their mission schools were the source of this new literacy learning. Māori for their part thought it absolutely wondrous that a man could be in one place, yet his written words could be read out loud in another as if he were present.

The increased contact between Māori and Pākehā inevitably led to conflict over land; different perspectives on property ownership; the debilitating effects of alcohol; and decimating diseases such as influenza, measles and syphilis. Some of the early Northland settlements – Kororāreka (now Russell) in particular – acquired a terrible reputation for drunkenness and general licentiousness. This situation eventually led to moves to establish a government and the rule of Western law.

THE TREATY OF WAITANGI AND NATIONHOOD

The office of British Resident was created in an attempt to establish governance; but without judicial powers and a supporting administration and, more importantly, without a military presence, the Resident filled a mediation role which proved less than satisfactory. However, in 1840 a group of northern chiefs signed a treaty document with the British Government which, in return for giving up their sovereignty over the country, promised them full citizenship and rights over their lands and resources.

In simple terms the Treaty of Waitangi, as it was known, established a government under a British governor, with the ability to make laws and administer the country. It has subsequently – but not without some controversy – become the nation's founding document.

Article the first [Article 1]
The Chiefs of the Confederation of the United Tribes of New Zealand and the separate and independent Chiefs who have not become members of the Confederation cede to Her Majesty the Queen of England absolutely and without reservation all the rights and powers of Sovereignty which the said Confederation or Individual Chiefs respectively exercise or possess, or may be supposed to exercise or to possess over their respective Territories as the sole sovereigns thereof.

Article the second [Article 2]
Her Majesty the Queen of England confirms and guarantees to the Chiefs and Tribes of New Zealand and to the respective families and individuals thereof the full exclusive and undisturbed possession of their Lands and Estates Forests Fisheries and other properties which they may collectively or individually possess so long as it is their wish and desire to retain the same in their possession; but the Chiefs of the United Tribes and the individual Chiefs yield to Her Majesty the exclusive right of Preemption over such lands as the proprietors thereof may be disposed to alienate at such prices as may be agreed upon between the respective Proprietors and persons appointed by Her Majesty to treat with them in that behalf.

Article the third [Article 3]
In consideration thereof Her Majesty the Queen of England extends to the Natives of New Zealand Her royal protection and imparts to them all the Rights and Privileges of British Subjects ■

CONFLICT WITH GOVERNMENT

The journey towards nationhood has been a troubled one for Māori and Pākehā. After the signing of the Treaty in 1840 a short but nasty war followed where the disaffected northern chiefs Hone Heke and Kawiti fought with the government in a conflict that included in its grievances the loss of trade opportunities and revenues through the relocation of the seat of government from the Bay of Islands to Auckland.

Fighting between Māori and the government then shifted south to the top of the South Island, and in the Hutt Valley near Wellington. In both locations the point of tension was the occupation by Pākehā settlers of land with disputed ownership.

When those tensions had ceased, race relations in this country entered a brief golden era, with Māori reaping the benefits of participation in the fledgling economy of the colony. The measure of success usually pointed to in the 1850s decade is the high number of grain mills and cargo ships in Māori ownership, trading as far afield as Australia.

The Ngāpuhi chiefs Hone Heke and Te Ruki Kawiti, shown dressed in traditional cloaks (and accompanied by Heke's wife Hāriata). The chiefs led Māori in the Northern Wars against the British in 1845–46.

Overwhelmed by new arrivals

All that came to a halt in the 1860s. Māori were overwhelmed by the rapaciousness of the settler need for land; and, most tellingly, by the end of the 1850s Pākehā for the first time had achieved numerical superiority. At the time of the signing of the Treaty in 1840 the ratio of Māori to Pākehā had been forty to one. But by the 1870s Māori were besieged as the new arrivals flooded the country. Māori security of mind, derived from the perceived comfort of being able to throw Pākehā back into the sea by sheer weight of numbers, had come to an end.

RESISTANCE AND RELIGION

The 1860s was a decade of war, beginning in Taranaki in 1860 and spreading to the Waikato and Bay of Plenty. Sporadic fighting continued into the 1870s, with the final subjugation of Māori resistance. By that time, their resistance had taken on the religious mantle that typifies the unequal struggle between an indigenous people looking for supernatural deliverance and a colonising power confident in the superiority of numbers and military technology.

Pai Mārire

The most telling manifestation of the search for supernatural assistance came in the rise of the Pai Mārire or Hauhau faith. The faith, with its millennial message that the heavenly host would come to the aid of Māori in the fighting and that the land would be restored to them as God had restored Canaan to the Jews, was derived from a Māori interpretation of the Bible and the gospel message. Some of the adherents to the faith were consumed by their beliefs, often entering a rapturous state in which they received prophecies conveyed to them by the wind. Their belief was such that they went into battle confident that they could ward off bullets by holding up their right hand, palm facing outwards.

Ringatū and Kīngitanga

Other late nineteenth-century independent religious movements arose from a similar rigorous examination and reinterpretation of the Bible. The most notable of these was the Ringatū faith, inspired by the guerrilla leader Te Kooti and, in the Waikato, Tariao. The Tariao faith was a further development of the Hauhau faith and was favoured by followers of a new political movement known as the Kīngitanga or Māori King Movement. Ringatū and Tariao carried the same message of supernatural aid from God and the restoration of the land, and both have endured into modern times.

The King Movement also survives. It was based on a desire by Māori to have their own king, who would share power with the English monarch under the one God. The King Movement also looked to halt the sale of Māori land by creating an aukati, a boundary, encompassing the lands of all the affiliated tribes and within which land sales were forbidden.

A depiction of the Ngāruawāhia headquarters of the Māori King in 1864, although by this time he was not in residence, having retreated south to the safety of the King Country.

DEFEAT AND LAND LOSS

In retrospect, what these various movements did was to provide Māori with time to adjust to the reality of defeat and to come to terms with the new world they now inhabited. The Māori population, which had been noticeably declining since 1856, went into steep decline after the 1860s wars. The reasons are again common to all indigenous peoples subject to the imposition of colonising government. Māori were a defeated people and suffered the economic and political helplessness that defeat brings, with the addition of rampant disease, poor health, lack of education and social dysfunction. As the century drew to a close there was some truth in an observation made by physician and politician Dr Isaac Featherston: 'A barbarous and coloured race must inevitably die out by mere contact with the civilised white … all we can do is to smooth the pillow of the dying Maori race'.

Chief among the fistful of reasons for the decline in Māori population at this time was the cultural wrench of being separated from their lands by either military confiscation or participation in questionable or dubious land sales. Other lands were compulsorily taken by the government for public works such as roads, railway lines and other infrastructure, for land survey costs, or for non-payment of rates (land taxes). These actions and deliberately legislated measures left Māori without the economic means to support themselves. Of all Māori grievances, land loss remains at the heart of the people's search for justice.

RESILIENCE AND GROWTH

The turn of the century brought a turn in fortunes for Māori. A group of energetic Māori politicians, the Young Māori Party, drove health, land and other reforms with the aim of improving health, housing and education opportunities for Māori. The early decades of the twentieth century can be depicted as a time of consolidation and of whakatipu, growth, including that of population.

A laughing group of Māori girls from 1910. They are probably a school group and are standing in front of a woven mānuka stick storage hut.

Children in front of the Rātana temple at Ohakune. The Rātana Church is an independent Māori Christian movement founded by the prophet Tahupōtiki Rātana in the 1920s.

The disruptions that came with the Boer War in South Africa and the First World War – where Māori served with distinction in the armies of the Empire – and then the Great Depression of the 1930s created hard times for Māori, but produced a tough and resilient people. There is little in the way of formal records that enable us to gauge the hardships that the Depression visited on Māori people, but the saving grace was probably that as a largely rural people they still depended on hunting and gathering for sustenance, and they generally led simple, uncomplicated lives.

The Rātana Church

It is from the 1920s that the last great Māori religious movement dates. The Rātana Church was founded by Tahupōtiki Rātana after a vision in which God spoke to him. As was the role of the earlier Christian-based Māori religious movements, the Rātana Church dispensed hope and faith at a time when people were oppressed and suffering from their economic burden.

The great disaster that disrupted this advance was the global conflict of the Second World War, when Māori people lost a generation of leaders to the battlefields of the world. It is a loss still felt today.

Prosperity for Māori – and indeed all New Zealanders – was the positive message from the buoyant economy of the 1950s, which rode along on the back

Playtime on the marae.

of high commodity prices for wool, butter, meat and timber and a secure market in the United Kingdom, with New Zealand filling the role of 'England's little farm'. As well, the many large government projects of those years – such as roading, railway construction, the building of hydroelectric dams and the expansion of the national forestry estate – provided many Māori families with full employment.

DRIFT TO THE CITIES

It is from this time that Māori began the significant migration that changed us from rural people to the urban people that we are today. The Māori urban migration has been largely driven by the search for employment; the implications of that migration have been far-reaching. For some Māori the move to the cities has resulted in links to the rural homeland being lost. The wholesale shift in population has also left many small country settlements much diminished, and the community life that revolved around home and marae subject to social fracture. Flashes of that community lifestyle are now apparent only at holiday time when families return to their ancestral homes to breathe life into their familial relationships.

Keeping in touch with the marae

Fortunately, New Zealand is a small country, and most settlements and marae are within reasonable driving distances of the main urban centres. Going to the 'home' marae for holidays, weekends and other occasions has become common, even though there is an economic cost attached to such visits which some find difficult to meet. There has been a consequent rise in the establishment of 'urban marae' – where membership is often community-based rather than hapū or iwi-based – but this rise does not compensate for the diminished rural communities in terms of people and ties, and membership of urban marae can sometimes mean that whānau and hapū ties are weakened accordingly.

The rise in the establishment of urban marae has also been driven by a desire to preserve the marae-related aspect of rural Māori life, and a desire by younger people to draw on the expertise within their urban communities by providing a familiar setting for the transmission of knowledge by urban kaumātua, elders. It is also the role of those kaumātua to encourage language use and the search for ancestral ties and links, fostering pride in their cultural heritage.

INTERMARRIAGE AND MIGRATION

The other major change, partly encouraged by the rural–urban shift, is that through Māori and Pākehā families living in closer proximity to each other it is quite common to find family members drawn from either ethnic group, and intermarriage is commonplace. The speed of this transition towards a more homogeneous population has been surprising. Most New Zealanders who are aware of their descent take pride in their Māori or Pākehā heritage.

In more recent years the hard economic times following the financial shocks to the global economy have meant that many Māori have joined a new employment migration – to Australia. Jobs are more easily obtained there, particularly in areas such as the mining industry; and higher wages, a common language and a shared Australasian culture make Australia an attractive proposition. Over 100,000 people of Māori ethnicity – one in six – now live in that country, and it's now rare to find a Māori family that does not have whānau members living and working there. The fear is that the 'Mozzies' – as Māori Australians are jokingly called – will lose touch with their cultural roots. Kapa haka (cultural performance) groups are found in most major cities in Australia, but it is inevitable that the full richness of Māori culture as it is still practised in New Zealand will be modified and aspects will be lost.

Others see this as an opportunity. Following the lead of the Māori culture group that has operated in London for decades – Ngāti Rānana ('the London tribe') – some Māori migrants view the reality of Māori in Australia as an opportunity to take aspects of the culture to a new frontier. ∎

CONTEMPORARY MĀORI SOCIETY

WHAT DOES MĀORI CULTURE in the twenty-first century look like? Surprisingly, many aspects of the traditional Māori society from which we have sprung still live on in modern life. The hierarchy of Māori society – whānau, hapū and iwi; family, extended family and tribe – remains largely intact. The institution of the extended whānau remains particularly strong, as does that of the hapū. Whānau and hapū are strengthened by the continuation of activities based on traditional facilities, the most important being the marae, which is still a central focus point for every Māori community around the country.

MARAE

The term marae still means an open space, the marae ātea, used for gatherings; but when Māori people talk about the marae nowadays they are usually referring to the entire modern marae complex rather than just the open space in front of the wharenui. The marae complex incorporates a number of separate elements that would have been present in only rudimentary form in traditional times.

The main element of the modern marae complex is the wharenui, literally the large house, but commonly referred to as the meeting house. The relatively small chiefly house of the past has evolved into a large building which lies very much at the heart of every Māori community. It is a cross between a community hall and church and is used for all kinds of gatherings involving whānau or hapū.

Most meeting houses are elaborately carved – for reasons of prestige – and are almost always named for an ancestral figure, usually the eponymous male ancestor of the hapū. The ancestor is said to be in a crouching position, with the ridge of the building representing his spine, the rafters his ribs and the amo or bargeboards on either side of the front of the building his arms, reaching down to embrace the people within his shelter.

The marae complex normally also includes a second building, the wharekai or dining hall. This building incorporates a kitchen and dining room and is of a size that can comfortably host visitors to the marae. It is normally named to commemorate a female ancestor. The modern marae complex will also have other buildings for ablutions, storage, administration and the like.

OPPOSITE TOP: *Wharenui, meeting house and urupā, cemetery at Waipiro Bay on the East Coast.*

OPPOSITE LOWER: *Te Takinga, Rotorua.*

CONTEMPORARY MĀORI RITUAL

The marae complex serves as the main setting and venue for the practice of cultural rituals. Once, those rituals provided a rich cultural patina to traditional Māori life, but today they are much reduced. For example, the old religious practices involved the use of karakia – chants or invocations; some would describe them as prayers – for most aspects of daily life. Karakia were largely designed to invoke the scenario that had successfully worked on a previous occasion. In this way it was expected that the ancestral gods would then favour the new endeavour because they had done so in the past. Appeals for supernatural assistance and protection through the proper recitation of the correct karakia are now practices largely lost to Māori. Where they survive it is usually the assistance of the Christian God that is invoked rather than the gods of our ancestors.

Nevertheless esoteric knowledge still survives with some individuals – tōhunga, adepts or experts. But the possession and practice of that knowledge is often beyond the needs of ordinary Māori people and their everyday lives. In a process that has been taking place steadily over the past 200 years, Māori spiritual values and accompanying rituals have been eroded and are in danger of becoming lost. Most ceremonial ritual has been replaced by adapted practices of the Christian faith, which denies deities other than the Holy Trinity, and this has made it almost impossible for the traditional modes of religious practice to be observed.

The transition towards a heavily influenced Christian ritual has been eased by the quick assimilation of Christian ritual by Māori. For example, early nineteenth-century Anglican, Wesleyan and Catholic religious forms were quickly placed in Māori contexts. Those cultural rituals that have survived in form, if not in content, and which feature in traditional Māori life may be divided into two groups: the rituals associated with the celebration of life; and those associated with death. ■

PŌWHIRI: ACCOMMODATING VISITORS

The pōwhiri is the ceremony most visitors to New Zealand with an interest in learning about Māori people, Māori culture and contemporary Māori life are likely to encounter.

In its traditional form the pōwhiri was designed to provide a transition whereby manuhiri, visitors, and strangers – whose motives for coming might be largely unknown and might therefore pose a potential physical or spiritual threat to their hosts – could be offered an opportunity to make clear their intentions and then, through a formal series of exchanges of information, gradually move to a point where they could become incorporated into the host group. The result was that both groups would become one people. They would then seal that joining together by sitting down and sharing food.

Nowadays a formal pōwhiri is normally reserved for special occasions or for welcoming important visitors.

BELOW: *The wero challenge is issued.*

OPPOSITE: *Women perform a light-hearted action song on the marae.*

Wero: challenge

The pōwhiri begins with the wero, or challenge. A warrior, usually armed with a taiaha, will step forward and issue a challenge on behalf of the hosts. The warrior will advance towards the visitors, leaping and weaving but forever alert and observant, while giving an athletic display of his prowess in the handling of the weapon and of his own abilities as a fighting man. At some pōwhiri there may be three such challengers.

The karanga of welcome is given as part of the pōwhiri.

While advancing, the warrior or warriors will be observing the guests to try to determine their intent. If the visitors' purpose is hostile they will send forward their own warriors with the intention of chasing and capturing the host challenger(s), thereby displaying their superiority. The challenging warrior must be able to elude these pursuers.

Offering and accepting a token

If the challenger determines that the visitors' intent is peaceful, he will lay down a small token in front of the visiting group. Originally, this token would have been a taki or wooden dart. Nowadays this has been replaced with a small stick or a leafed branchlet.

If the visitors pick up the token, this confirms that they come in peace.

Karanga: the women's call of welcome

Immediately the karanga – the women's call of welcome – breaks out. If the visitors have a kaikaranga in their midst, she will respond, telling the hosts who they are and why they have come. The women normally lead the way onto the marae; this is said by some to be a further indication that the visitors come in peace. The whole party pauses in front of the meeting house as a mark of respect before taking their seats – usually on the right-hand side of the marae as viewed from the wharenui. In an echo of the warrior past, only men sit in the front row of seats; and in an era of gender equality this arrangement is subject to continuing controversy.

Speech-making and singing

There then follows a series of alternating speeches from both sides; each speech embellished with a waiata, a song. The visitors' speeches might be wide-ranging in nature: they might first and foremost acknowledge those who have died in the interim since their last visit; then there might be explanatory comments about the nature or purpose of the visit, and further comments about the make-up of the visiting party. Only males are permitted to speak on the marae in this way, although females on extremely rare occasions may be given a speaking place.

At the conclusion of the visitor speeches, the last speaker may place a koha, a gift, on the marae. Formerly, the koha would have been food, but nowadays it is usually a sum of money, which represents the visitors' contribution towards the cost of the occasion. On some occasions the koha might receive its own karanga, and a person – normally male – is then delegated to go forward and retrieve the koha and thank the visitors for their generosity.

The host speeches, for their part, are usually welcoming in nature and might review events that have occurred since the two groups last met, as well as commenting on important matters affecting the marae and its people, or singling out particular individuals in the visiting party for special comment or mention. The hosts always end the speech-making by having the last word.

A speaker responds to speeches of welcome on behalf of a visiting group.

Greeting then sharing food and drink

The visitors are then invited to come forward and to meet the hosts with the hongi. This is a mode of greeting used only by Māori, whereby the participants gently press noses with each other, usually in one movement, but in some cases a double press is performed. The hongi is symbolic of the exchange of breath – which Māori regard as being the essence of life – and is normally accompanied by the harirū (literally 'how do you do') or handshake. The pōwhiri is then completed by hosts and visitors sitting down in the wharekai and sharing food and drink.

All visitors to a marae are termed to be waewae tapu, or under religious restriction. The purpose of the pōwhiri is to remove them from that state to a point where they can be one with their hosts; that is, they are subsumed and, for the duration of their stay on that marae, are regarded as being part of the marae and its people.

There may be slight variations to the pōwhiri ceremony described here, depending on the marae and what is regarded as being tikanga or proper practice for that particular hapū or iwi.

Whakatau

There is a short form of pōwhiri called the whakatau, which is for a less formal occasion and is often used in the form of an extended mihi or greeting. Use of the whakatau also avoids the cross-cultural clash that sometimes arises because women are prohibited from taking a speaking role on the open marae. The Māori view is that women, as the mothers of the iwi and therefore the carriers of the future, should be protected at all times – even from the verbal blows that might be delivered in the thrust and parry of marae debate.

RIGHT: *The hongi.*

OPPOSITE: *A large hui gathering gets under way on a marae.*

HUI: MEETINGS ON THE MARAE

The pōwhiri or whakatau is an important precursor to any hui or meeting held on the marae – or elsewhere; the protocol will usually be observed regardless of the hui venue. The cultural formalities that always precede engagement between Māori people are acutely observed, and they follow the same familiar pattern of moving people from a culturally unsafe state to one of safe inclusion by neutralising any tapu, spiritual danger, that might be brought by the visitors. Food is a neutralising agent, and for this reason it is also common practice for the hui participants to share refreshments immediately after the mihi is completed and before getting down to the kaupapa, the business at hand.

Hui cover an endless range of topics. The main reason for meeting on a marae is because the subject-matter is of interest to the people of that marae, or the hapū or iwi to which they belong; but equally there might be hui to discuss local council proposals, community health, education, land issues and so on. The protocols of hui are no different to any other meeting: someone usually chairs the meeting, someone keeps notes, and all have the right to a say and to one vote if needed.

Most hui end with a formal poroporoaki or farewell, complete with the recitation of karakia and the singing of a hymn. ■

Women mourners – the wearing of greenery on the head is usually a sign of mourning and grief.

TANGI: FUNERAL

As with all tribal peoples, for Māori the transition from life to death is about the beginning of a new journey. The rituals associated with that transition have evolved into a mixture of traditional and Christian elements that make the modern tangi – the Māori funeral – a unique event.

Sending the wairua on its journey

In traditional times when a person died their wairua – their spirit or soul, in Western terms – was said to remain nearby; and the purpose of proper ritual was to send the wairua on its journey so that it did not become an irritant to the living.

It was believed that the wairua returned to the Hawaiki homeland and that the departure point for its return journey was the northernmost tip of Te Ika a Māui, the North Island. Exactly what happened there is uncertain, but the next world was believed to be very much the same as this world except of course all the ancestors are there.

Journey to the home marae

Tangi ceremonial is similar to other Māori occasions where a religious context is appropriate. While such ceremonial is largely Christian in content it maintains an acknowledgement of a Māori concern for proper procedure: in this case karakia or prayers begin and end each phase of the ceremonies. Once a Māori person has died, their body is normally given over to an undertaker for preparation for burial. The deceased person is then returned to the family who, if they are associated with a marae, will organise for the funeral to take place there.

As Māori have increasingly become an urbanised people, death is seen as a reason for the return home to the kāinga, the home settlement, often in the rural heartland. This might require a journey of some distance, perhaps from as far as Europe but more usually from Australia. Bringing the dead 'home' is often seen as being an obligation on the family of the deceased.

Where the dead person and their family have lost their links to the 'home' marae, an urban marae will serve the purpose. In other cases, the deceased person with strong links to one place – through having lived there for many years or through marriage – might be briefly kept at the family home or taken on a short final visit to the local marae or urban marae to give those associated with the dead person an opportunity to pay their respects. The journey to the home marae will then proceed.

Karanga onto the marae

Members of the immediate family and of the hau kāinga, local community, will have gathered at the marae to prepare beforehand for the return of their dead kin. On arrival, the dead person and the accompanying party will be given a karanga onto the marae. The karanga at a tangi is almost always given by a woman, and her words are a mixture of grief and welcome to those arriving. If there are sufficient skilled members available, there may be a haka performed as the funeral party advances onto the marae. The normal haka used these days is 'Toia mai':

Tōia mai, te waka	Haul this canoe closer
Kūmea mai, te waka	Haul the canoe here
Ki te urunga i takoto ai	To the resting place
Te waka.	The canoe.

The waka or canoe is a reference to the coffin being carried by the pallbearers.

Sitting around the coffin

The coffin of the deceased person is usually placed in the centre of the back wall of the wharenui under the photographs of ancestors and family members who have passed away. The family of the deceased person arrange themselves around the coffin and the lid is removed. Everyone then sits – either on chairs provided for the occasion or on mattresses arranged around the walls of the wharenui.

Speeches and singing

The senior kaumātua present will then rise and speak. His speech will be a mixture of welcome and expressions of grief, and he will normally address the dead person directly. This first speech will sometimes contain a rebuke that the person has waited until death before coming home. The speech will contain some formal elements. For example, the dead person will be encouraged to takoto (lie here or pause here) kei roto i te aroha o te whānau (in the love of the family), but to then depart to te kāinga tuturu o ngā tāngata (the true home of people – usually interpreted as being the next world or the next life), to return to the ancestral homeland – Hawaiki nui, Hawaiki roa, Hawaiki pāmamao (great Hawaiki, long or extended Hawaiki, distant Hawaiki).

A family member or someone accompanying the funeral party might respond to this first speech. Others will then follow with similar messages and expressions of grief and sympathy. At the end of each such speech the speaker or others with him will sing a waiata, which may be a traditional song belonging to that particular location or hapū, or, as is becoming more prevalent these days, a waiata that is more generic and is known by many people so that others can join in.

Here is a lament belonging to the Ngāti Maru people where a widow laments the death of her husband and son:

> Tū tonu te rae, ē, i haere ai te makau
> E kai ana au, ē, i te ika wareware
> E aurere noa, ē, i te ihu o te waka.
> E kore hoki au, ē, e mihi ki a koe
> E mihi ana au, ē, ki a Ngahua te hoa
> Taku kāhui tara, ē, nō roto i au
> Tahu tōtara haemata, ē, nō roto no Moehau.
>
> ⸻
>
> Yonder stands the headland whence my loved one departed
> Wrapped in pleasant day dreams
> Sitting careless in the bow of the canoe.
> I do not mourn for thee so much my husband
> But I weep for Ngahua, my loved one
> My beautiful bird, my own offspring
> My stalwart young totara from the hills of Moehau.

Such a song might be sung with everyone appreciating that the sentiments expressed in the song, even though it is about another person and incident, are nevertheless applicable to the present sad occasion.

Sharing with hosts, and services

After the last speech from the hosts, the funeral party are invited to harirū, greet with the hosts. At the end of this phase there is usually a short Christian service of karakia and the singing of a hymn.

Through this informal ritual, as with the pōwhiri, the funeral party have had the tapu lifted off them and now become one with the hau kāinga, and all acknowledge that changed status by now sharing a meal together.

Later in the evening, after dinner, there will be a short service, a karakia (signalled by the ringing of a bell), with prayers, sometimes a scriptural message and a hymn. This marks the end of the formalities for the evening. This procedure will take place every night that the tangi continues.

The rest of the evening is mostly given over to families arranging bedding and sleeping spaces, looking after children, and catching up with others they haven't seen for some time, renewing family and friendship bonds. Others might take the opportunity now to say something to the deceased, or to their family in a more informal atmosphere.

Assisting with tasks

Meanwhile others will be in the kitchens preparing food, setting the tables, washing dishes, and all the other tasks that go into catering for large groups of people. The food gatherers may go hunting or fishing, gathering kaimoana (shellfish) and wild foods such as pūhā (sowthistle), watercress and any seasonal fruit that might be available. Some families will give food as their koha. It is normally the task of the bereaved family to provide workers to assist. A tangi

These days the hāngi meal often comes wrapped in foil.

is also a time for strengthening the ties of whānau and community, and that is best illustrated by the workers who give of their time voluntarily, knowing that there will be an occasion when they too will need the help of others.

The rituals of greeting

A tangi will normally proceed over three days to allow time for those wanting to attend to come from afar. A mourning party on arrival will normally gather at the waharoa, the gateway to the marae, which usually faces the marae wharenui. Their presence will be acknowledged and, once activities that are already happening in the wharenui or on the marae ātea are completed, the new arrivals will receive the karanga and be admitted to the marae grounds. The visiting women will lead their party onto the marae and will also respond to the karanga.

The rituals of greeting — speeches and waiata — are repeated for each successive group of visitors who are then enfolded into the grieving whānau and community. Speeches at tangi are often the setting for some of the best of Māori oratory. On the last evening of a tangi a special effort is made to have a particularly entertaining evening with much singing, storytelling, laughing and joking far into the night — sometimes right through until breakfast time.

Uncovering the hāngi – earth oven.

Two women greet with a hongi – gentle pressing of noses.

Concluding rituals: burial and feast

On the morning of the funeral service the immediate family are given one last chance to say their farewells before the coffin is closed. There is a final karanga poroporoaki and haka as the mourners leave the marae for the urupā, burial ground.

At the urupā there is a final service, and the grave is then filled. On leaving the urupā, because it is a tapu place, people rinse their hands with water to symbolically remove the tapu from their persons.

All return to the marae for the hākari, the feast which concludes all tangi. A special effort is made to provide a memorable meal with as many delicacies as the hosts are able to provide. Most of the meal is cooked in a hāngī, earth oven, which is ideal for cooking large quantities of food. The purpose of the feast is to demonstrate the whānau's gratitude for the sharing of their grief; and it is also an opportunity for the local people to show their prowess as hosts.

Hura kōhatu: headstone unveiling

The next event is the hura kōhatu or unveiling, which normally takes place about a year after the death. This ceremony replaces the pre-Christian practice of hahunga tūpāpaku, where the bones of the dead were gathered up, scraped clean of any residual flesh, carefully bundled and then secretly placed in their final resting place, which could be a rock crevice, a hollow tree or a cave. It was in many ways a celebration of the life of that person.

THE RENAISSANCE OF MĀORI CULTURE

IN NEW ZEALAND WE LOOK to Māori culture in so many ways to say something about us, who we are and where we come from. It gives an important point of difference between ourselves and other countries; and it has wide implications for tourism, sport, and the export and promotion of the country and New Zealand goods and services overseas. Despite the inroads of the Western world and foreign influence, Māori culture in New Zealand has undergone a renaissance and retains a vibrancy that ensures not just its survival but its continuing evolution and growth. This is attributable to several factors.

TE REO: THE MĀORI LANGUAGE

One of the most important factors in the revival and strengthening of Māori culture has been the energetic approach taken to the teaching and use of te reo, the Māori language. Māori is an official language of Aotearoa New Zealand, along with English and New Zealand sign language, and people are free to use it in forums such as the courts and the parliamentary debating chamber.

The Kōhanga Reo movement, which was behind the creation of total-immersion kōhanga reo (language nest) schools where young children are taught in Māori only, has been another vital component of this initiative. Other language revival agents have been the creation of the Māori Language Commission Te Taura Whiri i Te Reo Māori, with responsibility for overseeing the health and promotion of the language; and the establishment of the annual Māori Language Week in September each year. Ngā Manu Kōrero – the national secondary schools Māori speech competition – is another area that fosters the continuing growth and nurturing of the language.

KAPA HAKA: PERFORMING ARTS

At the same time, there has been a revival in Māori cultural performance. Some will say that it has never actually declined, and that is true to a point; but the spread of kapa haka – Māori song and dance – into many mainstream schools, and the fiercely contested national kapa haka competition Te Matatini, are

OPPOSITE TOP: *Māori children learn to speak te reo – the Māori language – under the Kōhanga Reo or language nest programme.*

OPPOSITE LOWER: *Members of a modern kapa haka group perform on the marae.*

ABOVE: *A woman performer sings while swinging the long poi as an accompaniment.*

ABOVE RIGHT: *A warrior performer joins the waiata or song.*

OPPOSITE: *Various types of flute – some of which are played by breathing into them through the nostrils.*

pointers to a healthy growth in interest and participation. In recent years kapa haka groups from Australia have also entered into the competition.

Kapa haka usually consists of group singing, poi performances, action songs – where the actions of the performers help tell the story of the lyrics – and haka. These days, kapa haka and singing occasions are normally accompanied by an acoustic guitar, although in the past, steel guitars, ukuleles, banjos, fiddles, harmonica, accordions and even Jew's harps have also featured.

Cultural performance makes an important contribution to the unique nature of not just Māori but New Zealand culture too. The Māori cultural presence is most notable in tourism, one of the major income generators in the New Zealand economy. Māori and Māori culture are very much the face of Aotearoa: apart from experiencing the New Zealand landscape in all its facets, the cultural experience that international visitors seek most is an engagement with Māori culture. Unfortunately, tight visitor schedules often mean that most of that engagement is of a cursory nature and is usually experienced as part of a cultural 'event' – for example, a visit to the thermal attractions of Rotorua, where Māori people provide guides and other services; or a cultural performance as part of the entertainment for a dinner.

MĀORI MUSIC

As you would expect with an oral society, performance plays an important role in the expression of Māori life and culture. Like other Pacific peoples, many Māori have a natural aptitude for cultural expression through singing, playing instruments or kapa haka.

Waiata

Traditional Māori singing sounds alien on first encounter because waiata are sung in what the untutored ear would describe as a monotone with the 'tune' often difficult to discern – a song could have an extremely small range, with tiny microtones contained within that range. The composition of traditional forms of waiata is becoming increasingly rare. A lot of Māori music in contemporary times follows Western forms such as hymns, or follows a popular practice that emerged during the Second World War of putting Māori words to a popular tune.

Instruments: taonga pūoro

Traditional Māori musical instruments – taonga pūoro – consisted mainly of trumpets, flutes, wooden gongs and whirled instruments (bullroarers). Stringed instruments were unknown in traditional times, but nowadays the guitar is the standard accompaniment for many Māori songs. The wooden drums found elsewhere in Polynesia and whose infectious beat is an important rhythmic dance accompaniment did not survive the transition to Aotearoa. The pahū (wooden gong), pūtātara (conch shell trumpet) and pūkaea (wooden trumpet) were used more as devices to sound a warning than as accompanying musical instruments. The only 'percussion' found in Māori music comes from the slap slap of poi, the small stringed balls used by poi dancers, hand claps in action songs, and the stamping of feet in the haka.

The most melodic of the taonga pūoro are the different flutes, which were played in various ways, including the kōauau or nose flute, played by breathing into it through the nostril. The music produced from these instruments is often described as plaintive. In modern times these flute instruments are normally played by experts and their playing has evolved into set-piece performances, an interesting musical development. These instruments have also taken on a specialist role rather than that of normal accompaniment to singing performances. The haunting music they produce is often a feature of film soundtracks that have a New Zealand setting. ∎

A kapa haka group performs a haka on Waitangi Day.

HAKA

Another cultural feature that has enjoyed a high international profile in recent years is the haka – best described as a warrior's challenge. Many New Zealand national sports teams perform the haka as part of their pre-match rituals. The haka is a physical challenge and a statement of intent that puts the opposition on notice that the contest to come is a serious one in which the participants will give of their best. Teams such as the All Blacks, New Zealand's world-famous rugby team, have made the haka an essential opener to any match against international rivals. The haka is an important part of the pre-match jousting by secondary schools, where it has become something of a tradition. It has also been adopted by other national teams representing organisations such as the Armed Services and the Police.

WAKA AMA

Hand in hand with the revival of Māori culture has been the revival of traditional activities, for example the sport of waka ama – outrigger canoe racing. In New Zealand, this sport is almost entirely a Māori domain, with intense competition at club, regional, national and international levels. Pacific Island nations – the Cook Islands and Tahiti in particular – are enthusiastic participants, and the competition engendered has helped cement the ties between Polynesian peoples as well as reviving a cultural tradition that had almost faded out.

Modern racing waka are very different machines to the traditional heavy, hollowed-out-log versions of former times. These are sleek fibreglass vessels that slide through the water, powered by the strong arms and bent backs of the crews. Competitions at the national level are highly organised, with racers divided into various categories based on age and gender. This sport has also gone Pacific-wide, with crews from Aotearoa competing in Rarotonga and Tahiti.

BELOW: *Fibreglass waka ama, contemporary Māori outrigger racing canoes. Competitive waka ama racing is one of the fastest growing sports among young and not-so-young Māori people.*

The modern ocean-going waka Te Matau a Māui, *which belongs to the Kahungunu people of the North Island, runs down the wind under full sail.*

Canoe voyaging

Separate from the high-energy buzz of waka ama racing is a more measured development: the revival of long-distance canoe voyaging. In recent years several seagoing vessels have been built using traditional designs, and have set sail using ancient instructions and methods – but with back-up technology such as GPS, for safety. This is a serene return to a time when sailing was more a test of survival skills and endurance, and time was not a driving motivation.

CONTEMPORARY TĀ MOKO

Aided by the use of modern tattoo implements, there has been an enormous increase in Māori (and indeed many other New Zealanders) acquiring face and body tattoos (moko) based on traditional Māori designs. The excruciating traditional process has been replaced by comparatively pain-free sessions. For many this might involve a simple design for the arms or legs; but the full-face moko design has made a comeback for men, and for women there has been a revival of the moko for chin and lips.

One other, sometimes unfortunate, feature of this Māori cultural renaissance has been the rapid global spread of Māori design concepts for use with tattooing.

The unique tattoo designs have been hugely popular, but many Māori see their use overseas as faddish and demeaning because the kōrero, the story, behind the tattoo design elements is ignored – usually because it is not known. Even worse, in the Māori view, is that the designs are not accorded the respect that they should be. Foreign tattoo artists who apply the designs have not bothered to learn those meanings or to take proper instruction.

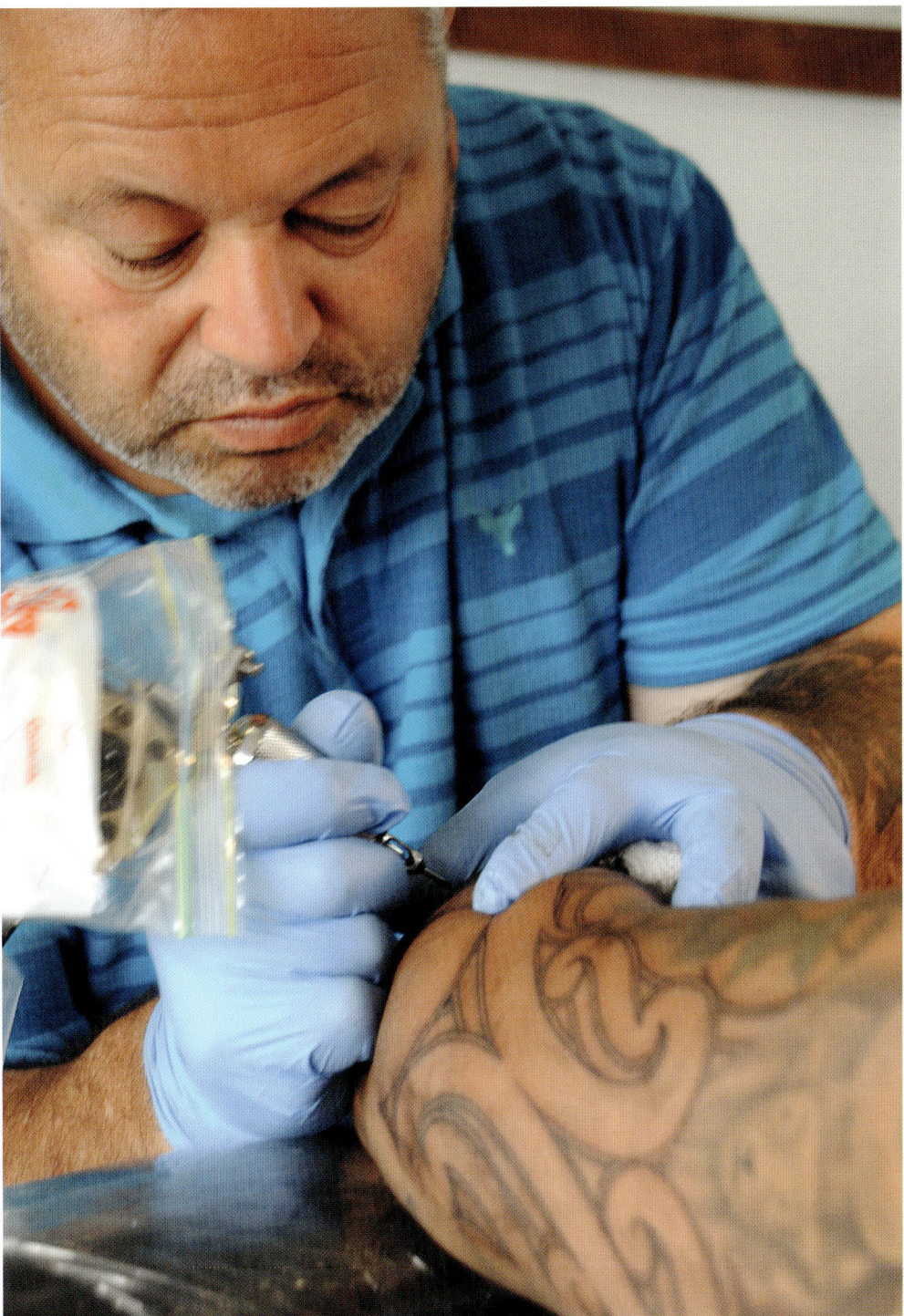

Master carver Riki Manuel undertaking moko (tattooing). Manuel is also renowned for his wood-carving works.

ART AND CRAFTS

Unlike many other indigenous peoples, in Māori culture, material arts and crafts – making things – survived into the contemporary world in relatively good health. One reason was the retention of rural links where items such as kete and kono – basketware and food containers – remained everyday domestic items and their manufacture continued largely unabated so that the skills of plaiting and weaving were kept alive.

Also, the demands of a burgeoning tourism industry meant the production of carved items of greenstone, shell, wood and bone for souvenirs. Traditional clothing such as piupiu (flax skirts) and kākahu (cloaks) were also produced for performance purposes. In recent times, new tools, techniques and materials have transformed small-scale art and crafts works made for the tourist market as well as major infrastructure works such as public memorials and many large art installations.

One event can be regarded as precipitating a global appreciation of traditional Māori art forms. The *Te Māori* exhibition opened at the New York Metropolitan Museum in 1984 and thereafter toured the world to much acclaim. The exhibition was a collection of some of the finest pieces of traditional Māori art held in the nation's museum collections. It confirmed what many Māori had always thought – that the art of their ancestors was not only stunningly dramatic but also had great aesthetic appeal. The applause of an international audience resounded loudly at home in New Zealand too, leading to a much greater appreciation of what Māori art has to offer in all its forms and reserving a place for Māori art as a unique flag bearer for national identity.

BELOW: *Kete – woven baskets displaying various designs of modern derivation.*

OPPOSITE: *clockwise from top left, pāua matau – fishhooks made from pāua (abalone) shell; a polished pounamu or greenstone pendant; flax weaving in progress; at the National Carving School at Te Puia in Rotorua, where aspiring Māori carvers learn from the masters. The figures carved are usually ancestors and the carving will contain visual clues to help identity of the ancestor as well as adding to the store of tribal stories depicted in a collection of such carvings. At Te Puia you can watch Māori carvers at work. The skills are passed from masters to students to ensure the ancient craft and stories stay alive in New Zealand.*

THE FUTURE

THERE WILL ALWAYS BE exceptions to the rule as with any other society, but as a general observation Māori remain a good people, kind, generous and normally of a sunny disposition. In this respect we are no different to our Polynesian brothers and sisters from all around the Pacific, and we carry with us still the traits and rhythms of our South Pacific heritage. Some think that we are fortunate to live in a country which to varying degrees has never stopped trying to overcome the inevitable economic gap that began in 1769 when the Stone Age that was the Māori world collided with the age of the Industrial Revolution – the technological and cultural cargo that the new settlers carried on board their ships.

In over 200 years of endeavour, while we have travelled far on our journey as a nation of two peoples, we have not yet achieved parity. We have the same wealth and poverty differentiations that are found in many other countries. Here, however, the people in the poverty group are mostly brown. At a time in world history when global events have created enormous instability in national economies and in the lives of ordinary people, it is those who are poorly equipped in terms of health, education and skills who are most affected.

Whatever happens to us as a nation and a people, there is one certainty, though: our Māori culture will survive. Too many Māori people have too much pride invested in it for the result to be anything other. It will be different from the culture that our ancestors brought here; evolution and the all-pervasive influence of the majority culture will see to that. It will have lost some of the layered richness that has sustained it over the centuries. But it will still be recognisable as different and unique in the world.

We shall never be lost, for are we not the far-flung seed of distant Rangiātea?

ABOVE: *Looking out to the world. View from near Te Rēinga at the northern tip of Aotearoa.*

LEFT: *Waka at Waitangi. Ngātokimatawhaorua is one of the world's largest ceremonial war canoes. The hull is carved from two massive kauri trees, felled in the Puketi Forest in Northland.*

OPPOSITE: *Contemporary carvings wrought in concrete outside the New Zealand Parliament in the capital city of Wellington.*

APPENDIX A: THE NATIONAL ANTHEM

The resurgence of Māori and Māori culture in the past twenty years is brilliantly illustrated by the adoption and incorporation of a Māori verse at the start of the national anthem. Most New Zealanders – certainly all young people – know and sing both versions of the first verse.

Māori verse: Aotearoa	English verse: God Defend New Zealand
E Ihowā Atua,	God of Nations at Thy feet,
O ngā iwi mātou rā	In the bonds of love we meet,
Āta whakarangona;	Hear our voices, we entreat,
Me aroha noa.	God defend our free land.
Kia hua ko te pai;	Guard Pacific's triple star
Kia tau tō atawhai;	From the shafts of strife and war,
Manaakitia mai	Make her praises heard afar,
Aotearoa.	God defend New Zealand.

APPENDIX B: THE 'KA MATE' HAKA

One of the best-known haka is 'Ka Mate', regularly performed by national sporting teams. 'Ka Mate' was composed by Ngāti Toa chief Te Rauparaha around 1820, when he was being pursued by enemy warriors. It tells the story of the fear of capture and exhilaration of survival. Here is the best-known verse:

Ā, ka mate! Ka mate! Ka ora! Ka ora!	It is death! It is death! It is life! It is life!
Ka mate! Ka mate! Ka ora! Ka ora!	It is death! It is death! It is life! It is life!
Tēnei te tangata pūhuruhuru	There stands the hairy man
Nāna nei i tiki mai whakawhiti te rā	Who will cause the sun to shine
Ā, upane! ka upane!	A step upwards, another step upwards!
Ā, upane! ka upane! Whiti te rā!	A step upwards, another step upwards. The sun shines!

GLOSSARY

Pronunciation: Every vowel is given its full sound. A macron (e.g. ā) over a vowel indicates a long sound. Vowel sounds: 'a' as in star – sounds like aaah…; 'e' as in feather – like air…; 'i' as the 'e' in English; 'o' as in door – like oar; 'u' as the long double 'o' in ooze. With consonants: 'r' is rolled slightly; 'p' is a soft p. There are two diphthongs: 'wh' and 'ng' – 'wh' is pronounced like the English 'f'; 'ng' is like the middle 'ng' in singing.

amo	bargeboards
Aotearoa	the Māori name for New Zealand; loosely translated as 'The Land of the Long White Cloud'. It also traditionally referred to the North Island.

ariki	person with the most senior descent line in the tribe and acknowledged as the leading chief (rangatira) – could be male or female
atua	in the traditional world, a deity or (ancestral) god
aukati	boundary, border
aute	paper mulberry (*Broussonetia papyrifera*), brought to New Zealand by Māori; but did not survive here
hahunga tūpāpaku	a traditional ceremony when the bones of the dead were cleaned and mourned over one more time before final disposal
haka	posture dance; a general term for several types of vigorous dances with actions and rhythmically shouted words
hākari	feast
hāngī	earth oven to cook food with steam and heat from heated stones
hapū	a collection of extended families (whānau) with a common ancestry sometimes deemed to be a subtribe
harakeke	native flax (*Phormium tenax*)
harirū	handshake
hau kāinga	the 'home' people
Hawaiki	not a locatable place, but the name that seems to have been always given to the last departure point from the ancient homeland of voyagers from the Pacific Islands. It survives in the dialects of the Pacific peoples; other variants are Hawai'i (for the place of the same name), and Savai'i, the island in Western Samoa.
hoe	canoe paddle
hongi	pressing of noses (and hence an exchange of breath) as a form of a greeting
hue	gourd (*Lagenaria siceraria*) brought to New Zealand by Māori
hui	meeting or conference
hura kōhatu	ceremony surrounding the unveiling of a headstone at a gravesite
iwi	tribe
kaikaranga	the woman (or women) with the role of making the ceremonial call to visitors onto a marae, or equivalent venue, at the start of a pōwhiri
kaimoana	seafood, shellfish
kāinga	hamlet or small undefended settlement; sometimes refers to home
kākahu	cloak, garment
kapa haka	Māori song and dance performance
karakia	invocations – but through general usage has come to mean prayer
karanga	the woman or women's call of welcome or response on entering onto a marae
kaumātua	elder – usually refers to a male
kaupapa	topic or subject or reason for a hui
kete	basket or kit
kiore	Polynesian (or Pacific) rat (*Rattus exulans*), brought to New Zealand by Māori; also refers to any rat or mouse
kōauau	nose flute, played by breathing into it through the nostril
koha	gift, normally money

kōhanga reo	'language nests' – preschools where all teaching is in the Māori language
kono	small basket or kit for containing food, especially cooked food
kōrero	talk, story, narrative
kōwhaiwhai	painted scroll ornamentation, commonly used on meeting house rafters
kūmara	sweet potato (*Ipomoea batatas*), brought to New Zealand by Māori
kurī	small Polynesian dog (*Canis lupus familiaris*), brought to New Zealand by Māori, now extinct; also refers to any dog
mana	prestige
manuhiri	visitors, guests
mānuka	tea-tree (*Leptospermum scoparium*), a common shrub or small tree with aromatic, prickly leaves and many small white, pink or red flowers
Māori	the indigenous people of New Zealand
marae	shortened form of marae ātea, which describes the flat open space immediately in front of the principal building within a settlement. In modern times it has come to be the name used to describe the collection of buildings which make up a marae complex.
marae ātea	the flat open space immediately in front of the principal building within a settlement; *see* marae
matau	fishhook
mere	short-handled bladed striking club
mihi	greeting or welcome – sometimes describes a short speech of welcome
moa	native giant flightless bird (*Dinornis* and five other genera), now extinct
moko	tattoo pattern – usually facial, but may refer to body tattoo also
nīkau	native palm (*Rhopalostylis sapida*)
pā	fortified village
pāhu	wooden gong
Pākehā	New Zealanders of European descent
pātaka	storehouse
patu	club (weapon)
pāua	abalone (*Haliotis* species), edible univalve molluscs of rocky shores.
pipi	a common edible bivalve with a smooth shell found in sandy harbour flats
piupiu	a type of skirt made of flax used today for kapa haka performances
poi	small balls of woven flax and raupō on strings and used as a song accompaniment
poroporoaki	speech of farewell
pou	post, pole (often carved)
pounamu	greenstone or New Zealand jade
poupou	carved wall figures
pōwhiri	ceremony of welcome
proa, prau	double-hulled sailing canoe – still sailed in Micronesia
pūhā	sowthistle (*Sonchus* species)
pūhoro	upper thigh (or arm) tattoo pattern

pūkaea	wooden trumpet
pūkeko	native purple swamphen (*Porphyrio porphyrio*)
pūtātara	shell trumpet normally made with a conch shell
rangatira	chief or gentleman
raperape	buttocks tattoo pattern
raupō	native bulrush (*Typha orientalis*)
tā moko	applying a tattoo; the practice of Māori tattooing
taiaha	thrusting quarterstaff
taki	small wooden dart
tangata whenua	indigenous people, local people, hosts
tangi	funeral
tao	spear
taonga pūoro	musical instruments
tapa	the beaten bark of the aute or paper mulberry bush used to make a rudimentary cloth
tapu	sacred, prohibited, restricted, set apart, forbidden
taro	swamp-growing plant (*Colocasia esculenta*) known throughout the Pacific and whose starchy root is eaten as a staple food item
taua	war party
tauihu	canoe prow – often bearing a carved figure or figures
tauiwi	foreigner(s)
taurapa	canoe stern piece – usually highly carved
Te Ika a Māui	the North Island of New Zealand
tewhatewha	long-handled club
tihi	tip or highest point
tikanga	proper practice or protocol
toheroa	a large edible bivalve with a triangular shell found in fine sand between tides
tōhunga	an adept, expert or master
tōtara	native tree of the *Podocarpus* genus – much favoured by Māori as a building and carving timber
tuangi	cockle (bivalve), found in tidal mudflats and sand-flats
tukutuku	ornamental latticework, used particularly between carvings around the walls of meeting houses
urupā	burial ground
utu	revenge
waewae tapu	visitors – literally 'those with sacred feet'
waharoa	gateway or entranceway to a marae complex
waiata	song
wairua	spirit or shade, but now used as a synonym for soul
waka	canoe
waka ama	outrigger canoe or the sport of outrigger canoe racing

waka taua	war canoe
weka	native woodhen (*Gallirallus australis*)
wero	warrior challenge as part of a formal pōwhiri ceremony
whakairo	wood carving
whakatau	informal greeting ceremony
whakataukī	proverb or saying
whakatipu	to grow, including in population
whānau	extended family
wharekai	dining hall
wharenui	'large house' – the principal building in a marae complex
wheke	octopus

COMMON GREETINGS

Kia ora	Hello	**Tēnā koutou**	Hello (more than two people)
Kia ora koe	Hello (you – one person)	**Hei konei rā**	Goodbye
Kia ora kōrua	Hello you two	**Ka kite anō**	See you later
Kia ora koutou	Hello everybody	**Haere rā**	Farewell
Tēnā koe	Hello (one person)	**Haere rā koutou**	Farewell to you all

IMAGE CREDITS

Adrienne Rewi: front cover (lower left), rear cover (lower); text pp. 2–3, 4–5, 7 (top, lower left & right), 8 (top & lower), 11 (top), 14, 16, 18, 19 (left & right), 20 (lower), 35 (top & lower), 47, 49 (top), 50 (left & right), 51, 53, 54, 55, 56, 57 (top left, top right, centre), 58.

Alexander Turnbull Library, Wellington, New Zealand: p.13 (top) PUBL-0015-09, p.13 (lower) PAColl-7273-03, p.15 PA1-o-042-19-2, p.17 (top) PAColl-7985-84, p.17 (lower) 1/1-006227-G, p.21 A-080-012, p.22 1/4-021668-F, p.23 PA1-o-042-12-1, p.25 E-453-f-001, p.26 B-088-004, p.28. C-012-019, p.29 E-047-q-009, p.30 1/1-007526-G.

Destination Rotorua Marketing: p.57 (bottom).

James Heremaia: front cover (bottom centre & lower right); text p. 59 (lower).

Maori Tourism: front cover (top), rear cover (top left & right); text pp. 9, 11 (lower), 20 (top), 27, 31, 32, 36, 37, 38, 39, 40, 41, 42, 45, 46, 49 (lower), 59 (top).

Rui Camilo: p.54 © Rui Camilo – www.rui-camilo.de; Pacific Voyagers – www.pacificvoyagers.org.

Shutterstock: p.52 136949045 © ChameleonsEye.

Treaty House, exhibition in the South Wing. Image used with permission of Waitangi Treaty Grounds, p. 27.